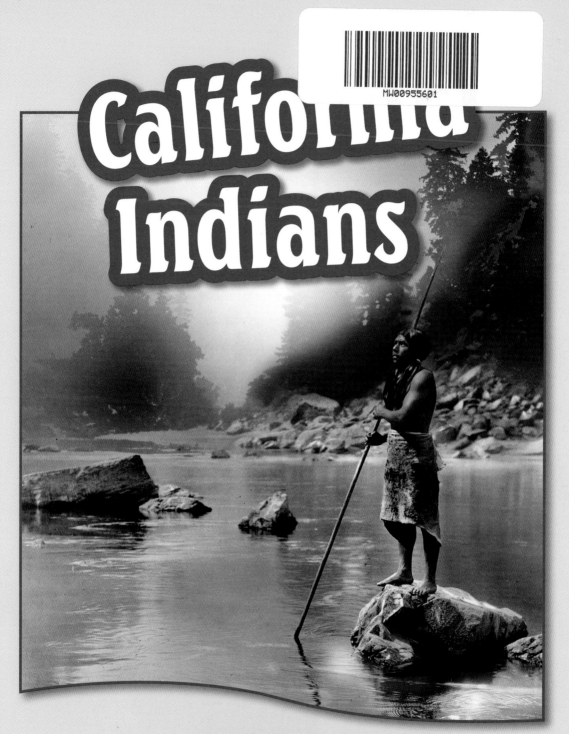

# California Indians

**Ben Nussbaum**

## Consultants

**Crystal Hahm, M.A., Ed.M.**
*Tustin Unified School District*

**Bijan Kazerooni, M.A.**
*Chapman University*

### Publishing Credits

Rachelle Cracchiolo, M.S.Ed., *Publisher*
Conni Medina, M.A.Ed., *Managing Editor*
Emily R. Smith, M.A.Ed. *Series Developer*
June Kikuchi, *Content Director*
Susan Daddis, M.A.Ed., *Editor*
Courtney Roberson, *Senior Graphic Designer*

**Image Credits:** front cover, p.1LOC, LC-cph 3c13079; p.2 LOC, LC-cph 3c01257; p.6 LOC, LC-cph 3c36570]; p.8 (bottom) National Geographic Creative/Alamy; pp.8–9 (top) Spencer Weiner/Los Angeles Times via Getty Images; p.10 Danita Delimont/Alamy; p.11LOC, LC-cph 3b45699; pp.12–13 (top) Luis Sinco/Los Angeles Times via Getty Images; p.13 (top) LOC, LC-cph 3c13079; p.14 (insert) USC Libraries Special Collections (CHS-3803); p.15 (bottom) USC Libraries Special Collections (CHS-3795); pp.16–17 LOC, LC-cph 3c20023; p.17 (insert) Bobbi Onia/Underwood Archives/Getty Images; p.19 (bottom right) LOC, LC-ppmsca 08116; p.20 (bottom) Lonely Planet/Getty Images; p.22 National Archives and Records Administration; p.23 LOC, LC-ppmsca 18212; p.24 Irfan Khan/Los Angeles Times via Getty Images; p.25 LOC, LC-PDF 36026283; p.26 (insert) Kilmer Media/Shutterstock; p.27 Kobby Dagan/Shutterstock; p.31 LOC, LC-cph 3c10505; all other images from iStock and/or Shutterstock.

**Library of Congress Cataloging-in-Publication Data**

Names: Nussbaum, Ben, 1975- author.
Title: California Indians / Ben Nussbaum.
Description: Huntington Beach, CA : Teacher Created Materials, [2018] | Includes index. | Audience: Grades K-3.
Identifiers: LCCN 2017053307 (print) | LCCN 2017056326 (ebook) | ISBN 9781425825621 | ISBN 9781425825201 (pbk.)
Subjects: LCSH: Indians of North America--California--Juvenile literature.
Classification: LCC E78.C15 (ebook) | LCC E78.C15 N86 2018 (print) | DDC 979.4/00497--dc23
LC record available at https://lccn.loc.gov/2017053307

### Teacher Created Materials

5301 Oceanus Drive
Huntington Beach, CA 92649-1030
www.tcmpub.com

**ISBN 978-1-4258-2520-1**

# Table of Contents

# A Diverse Land

California is a state made up of different land features. Its coast is beautiful. It goes on and on. The Central Valley is huge. It is flat and **fertile**. The desert is harsh. It can seem totally empty. In many areas of the state, mountains seem to climb to the sky.

In the past, California Indians lived in each of these places. Some tribes lived in big houses in large villages. Other tribes lived in tiny groups and moved often. Tribes near the sea ate fish. Some tribes ate insects gathered from the shallow water of mountain lakes. Others walked around the desert, searching for blooming cacti.

Each tribe had its own way of life. Each tribe had its own stories and beliefs.

## Mono Meal

The Mono tribe ate alkali fly **pupas** (PYOO-puhs). The worm-like pupas were a great source of fat and protein. The pupas could also be dried and stored for eating later.

# The Comfy Coast

Many tribes lived along California's coast. Most of the time, the weather was mild. The ocean provided food and other **resources**. Land a few miles away from the ocean was valuable, too. It was often fertile, with rivers and streams.

The ocean gave tribes many things to use. It also gave them many things to trade. Tribes dried fish, gathered salt, or collected rare shells. They traded these items for things such as nuts and deer pelts. California Indians all over the state **bartered**. People within a tribe traded with each other. Tribes bartered with other tribes. Items could change hands many times.

A California Indian uses a net to catch fish.

California coastline

## A Long Journey

People as far away as Utah used shells from the Pacific Ocean. The shells were used as decorations. They had to be traded many times to get that far.

People on the coast had many ways to get food from the ocean. They ate whales that washed up on the shore. Or, they caught fish in the tide.

The Chumash (CHOO-mash) and Tongva (TON-vah) tribes lived in the southern part of the state. They built tomols, a type of canoe. With their sturdy tomols, boating was part of their daily lives.

Tomols were made from wood that washed up on the beach. People cut the wood into **planks** using bones or antlers. They glued the planks together. Then, they tied the planks together with rope made from plants. Finally, they poured tar over the cracks. A single tomol could take six months to build.

Chumash Indians carry a tomol ashore.

Modern Chumash Indians share their culture by building and using a tomol.

## Thunder and Lightning

The Chumash told folktales to explain things that happened in nature. One tale told of two brothers who lived in the "upper world." They liked to play the hoop-and-pole game. One brother rolled the hoop. The other boy ran after it to hit it with his pole. That caused thunder. They also had the ability to throw light. That is how these early people explained lightning!

# The Mighty Mountains

In mountain areas, food was harder to find. People moved often and lived in small groups.

Some mountain tribes were feared by their neighbors. Some had a reputation for being warlike. They did not live in big villages. They did not own many things. It was easy for them to raid tribes in low-lying areas and then hide.

In other mountain areas, flat valleys or lakes made life easier. People were more settled. They had more stable lives.

The Hupa (HOO-pah) tribe lived in the Hoopa Valley near Oregon. The Trinity River provided the Hupa with water and fish. The Hupa built villages on flat land next to the river.

Cedar planks were used by the Hupa to build houses and storage buildings.

## Big Fish

The Hupa sometimes fished for sturgeon. These fish can grow up to seven feet (2 meters) long and can weigh hundreds of pounds!

This Hupa Indian fishes from a platform using a net.

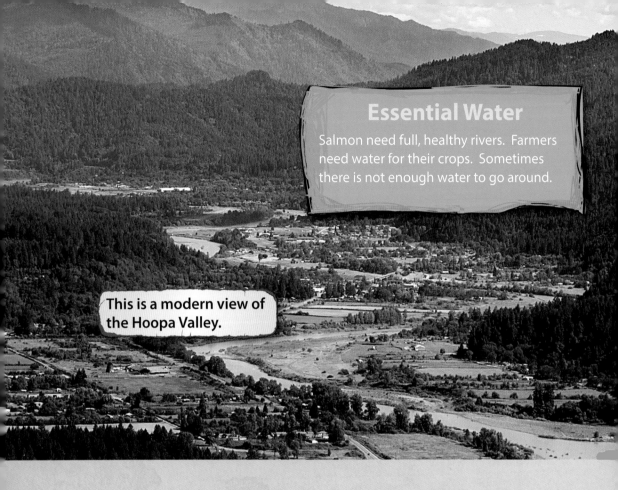

### Essential Water

Salmon need full, healthy rivers. Farmers need water for their crops. Sometimes there is not enough water to go around.

This is a modern view of the Hoopa Valley.

The **staple** food for the Hupa was salmon. Each spring, the Hupa had a ceremony to welcome the salmon back to the river.

This was known as the first-salmon ceremony. Other tribes had first-salmon ceremonies, too. First, a fish was caught. Next, it was sprinkled with valuable things, such as eagle **down**. After it was cooked, each member of the tribe ate a small piece of the fish.

Mountain tribes were lucky, in a way. For a long time, settlers did not want the mountain land. It was not good for farming. Because of this, some tribes that lived in the mountains were not pushed off this land. The Hupa still live in the Hoopa Valley.

A Hupa Indian readies his spear.

Salmon are born in freshwater but live most of their lives in saltwater.

# The Valuable Valley

The Central Valley is a large place with some of the best soil in the world. It makes the land fertile, green and full of life. People around the world feast on fruits and vegetables from the Central Valley.

The Yokuts (YO-koots) tribe lived in the southern part of the valley. Areas in the valley were very wet, with swamps and marshes. Yokuts ate **waterfowl**, such as geese and ducks. They ate deer and elk that lived on the edges of marshes. They also ate fish, turtles, roots, and seeds. And they ate acorns like other California Indians did all over the state.

Tule (TOO-lee) grew all over the valley. This **reed** was a huge part of the tribe's daily life. They made baskets and boats from tule and ate its roots.

A Yokuts Indian weaves a basket.

Different types of deer can be found throughout California today.

## Dozens of Dialects

The Yokuts tribe was made up of about 50 small groups. Scholars call these groups *tribelets*. Each tribelet had its own version of the Yokuts language!

Yokuts women and children slice and remove pits from peaches.

Yokuts villages were normally large. One type of home was made by curving sticks into dome shapes. The sticks were then covered with mats made from tule.

Some Yokuts homes were so big that many families lived in them. Each family had its own door and fireplace, but there were no inside walls.

Each Yokuts village also had a sweathouse. It was made with wooden planks covered with brush and dirt. A fire kept the building hot.

Both Yokuts and Hupas built sweathouses.

Women used the sweathouse sometimes, but it was mostly for men. They used it as a gathering place. They told stories and sang. There were nights when men even slept in it. Sweathouses were an important part of village life in many areas of the state.

Yokuts build a frame for a house.

# The Difficult Desert

The desert was a hard place to live. The summers were very hot while the winters were brutally cold. There weren't many plants or animals for food.

The Quechan (kwuh-TSAHN) tribe lived in the desert. The Quechan were farmers, which was very unusual for tribes that lived in this part of the state.

## Awesome Agave

The agave (uh-GAH-vay) plant was very important for people who lived in the desert. It could be cooked and eaten many different ways. Its fibers were used for shoes and clothes.

They lived above the **floodplain** of a river. When the river flooded, it left rich, wet land behind. The Quechan moved closer to the river and planted **maize**, melons, and other plants. They took care of the plants as they grew. This was one strategy for getting food in the desert!

This Quechan musician is covered in body paint.

The Coso (KOH-soh) people lived in and near the Coso Range. In this area, desert and mountains mix. It is hot and dry. There are few animals and plants.

One good thing about the Coso Range is that it has obsidian (uhb-SIH-dee-ihn). This is a type of glass made when lava melts. Obsidian can be chipped into very sharp blades. Coso Range obsidian was used by many tribes in the state.

There were not many people in the Coso tribe. They lived in small villages near the few sources of water in the desert.

The Coso Range is full of rock art. It depicts people, animals, and abstract shapes. It was made by the Coso and also by tribes that lived in the area before them.

Pictures of bighorn sheep are carved into some rocks at Coso Range.

**Fossil Falls is part of the Coso Range.**

## A Better Blade

Obsidian knives are so sharp that a small number of doctors still use them for surgery. An obsidian knife leaves a smaller scar than a steel knife. The cut heals faster, too.

# Safe Places

In the 1500s, Europeans began exploring the West Coast. Some people settled in the region. They brought new diseases. They cut down forests. They drained lakes. Their pigs and cows destroyed native plants.

Life changed for tribes in California. The Spanish enslaved them. Many tribes were forced to move. They had to work and live on **missions**. The Spanish killed many native people, too.

Over time, attitudes changed. In 1906, the state began to buy land. The land was set aside for California Indians to live.

Today, there are many of these places in the state. Some of these places are called *rancherias*. They tend to be smaller pieces of land. The rest are called *reservations*, which are larger.

A young California Indian from a rancheria helps pick grapes.

## Mission History

When the Spanish settlers came, they built missions. Many California Indians were forced to live and work on these missions. During that time, 21 missions were built. Today, you can travel over 600 miles (965 kilometers) to see the missions along the coast.

Mission San Diego was the first mission built by the Spanish people.

A high school basketball team practices on their reservation.

Rancherias and reservations are unique places. People in a tribe can live together. They can make their own laws. They can have their own police force.

Many tribes have constitutions. These documents say who can be members of their tribes. Rules are set for tribes to follow. For example, constitutions outline how leaders are elected.

Tribes are like small nations. In part, this is because of **treaties** signed long ago. These treaties say tribes can govern themselves.

People in a tribe are also citizens of the country. The state government does not have very much control over tribes. But the U.S. government does. It can set limits on how much freedom tribes have.

## CONSTITUTION AND BYLAWS OF THE TULE RIVER INDIAN TRIBE OF CALIFORNIA

### PREAMBLE

We, the members of the Tule River Bands of the Tule River Indian Reservation in the State of California, in order to establish our tribal organization, to conserve our tribal property, to develop our community resources, to administer justice, and to promote the welfare of ourselves and our descendants, do hereby ordain and establish this constitution and bylaws of the Tule River Indian Tribe, to serve as a guide for the deliberations of our tribal council in its administration of tribal affairs.

### ARTICLE I—TERRITORY

The jurisdiction of the Tule River Indian Tribe shall extend to the territory within the confines of the Tule River Indian Reservation, situated in Tulare County, State of California, as established by Executive orders of January 9 and October 3, 1873, and of August 3, 1878, to all lands claimed by the tribe and to which title in the tribe may hereafter be established; and to such other lands as may hereafter be added thereto under any law of the United States, except as otherwise provided by law.

### ARTICLE II—MEMBERSHIP

SECTION 1. The membership of the Tule River Tribe shall consist of the following:

(a) All persons of Indian blood whose na-

# Past, Present, and Future

One way to honor the past is to learn more about it. There are many ways to find out about the state's first people. Museums have artifacts on display. You can see old tools and baskets. Libraries and parks sometimes display artifacts, too. All over the state, tribes share their old ways of life. They teach dances and songs.

There are other ways to learn more about the future of the state's first people. Tribes welcome visitors to festivals and **powwows**. You can explore modern food and modern art of different tribes.

Learn about issues that are important to tribes. They are growing stronger but still face challenges. Discover what you can do to help!

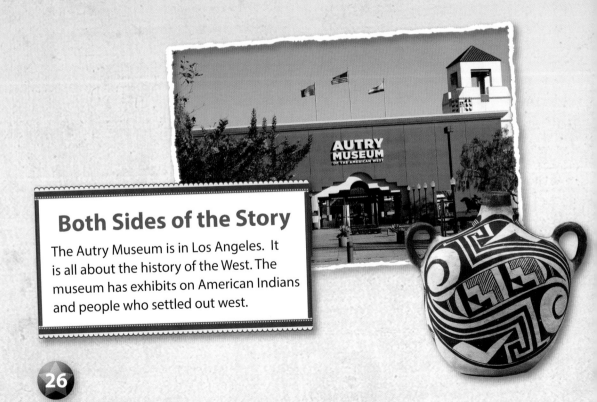

### Both Sides of the Story

The Autry Museum is in Los Angeles. It is all about the history of the West. The museum has exhibits on American Indians and people who settled out west.

American Indians participate in a powwow to share their culture.

# Bury It!

American Indian artifacts are things left behind by people of the tribes. They show how American Indians lived. Arrowheads, fishhooks, and bowls are important artifacts. Scholars can figure out a lot from a small artifact!

Artifacts are things that last a long time. Some artifacts are thousands of years old. Think about the things you use. What are some things that would make great artifacts?

Make a time capsule. Find a good container that will last a long time. Put a few items in it that will last a long time, too. Bury the time capsule at home or at school.

If someone finds it a hundred years from now, what can they discover about you?

# Glossary

**bartered**—traded one thing for another instead of selling something for money

**down**—a type of feather, usually from geese

**fertile**—capable of supporting the growth of many plants

**floodplain**—low, flat land that may flood

**maize**—corn

**missions**—places or buildings where religious work is done

**planks**—pieces of wood cut into long, skinny boards, used for building

**powwows**—American Indian ceremonies and get-togethers, often with dancing and food

**pupas**—young insects in the stage between larva and adult

**reed**—a long, thin, grass-like plant

**resources**—things that are usable

**staple**—a most important food

**treaties**—formal agreements made between two or more countries or groups

**waterfowl**—birds that live near bodies of water, like ducks and geese

# Index

# Your Turn!

## CONSTITUTION AND BYLAWS OF THE TULE RIVER INDIAN TRIBE OF CALIFORNIA

### PREAMBLE

We, the members of the Tule River Bands of the Tule River Indian Reservation in the State of California, in order to establish our tribal organization, to conserve our tribal property, to develop our community resources, to administer justice, and to promote the welfare of ourselves and our descendants, do hereby ordain and establish this constitution and bylaws of the Tule River Indian Tribe, to serve as a guide for the deliberations of our tribal council in its administration of tribal affairs.

### ARTICLE I—TERRITORY

The jurisdiction of the Tule River Indian Tribe shall extend to the territory within the confines of the Tule River Indian Reservation, situated in Tulare County, State of California, as established by Executive orders of January 9 and October 3, 1873, and of August 3, 1878, to all lands claimed by the tribe and to which title in the

## Classroom Constitution

A constitution is a set of rules that directs how a group of people will work together. The constitution above describes how the Tule tribe governs and lives. Create a classroom constitution. What rules are needed to keep an orderly and fair classroom for teachers and students? Write at least three rules using language that sounds official.